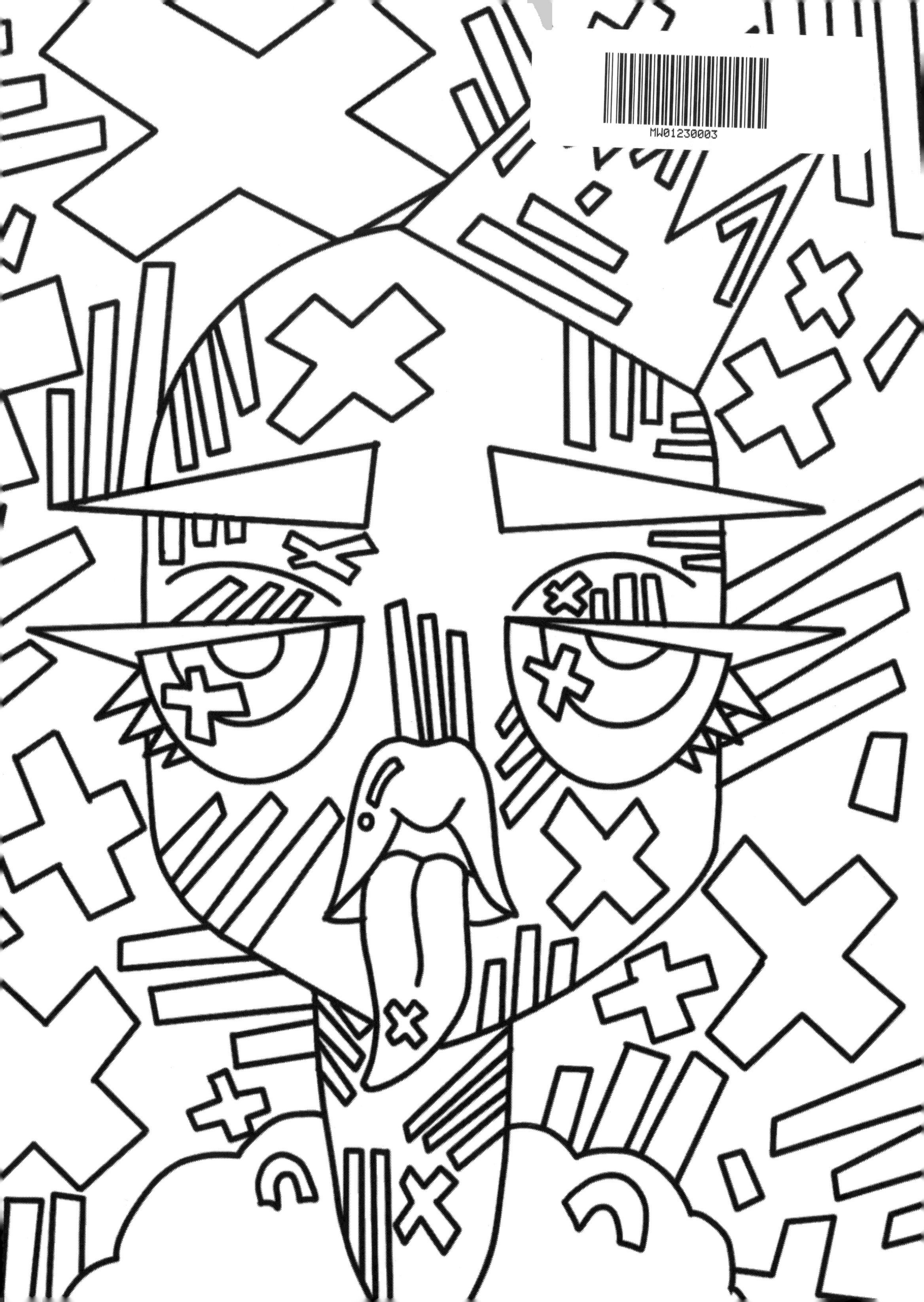

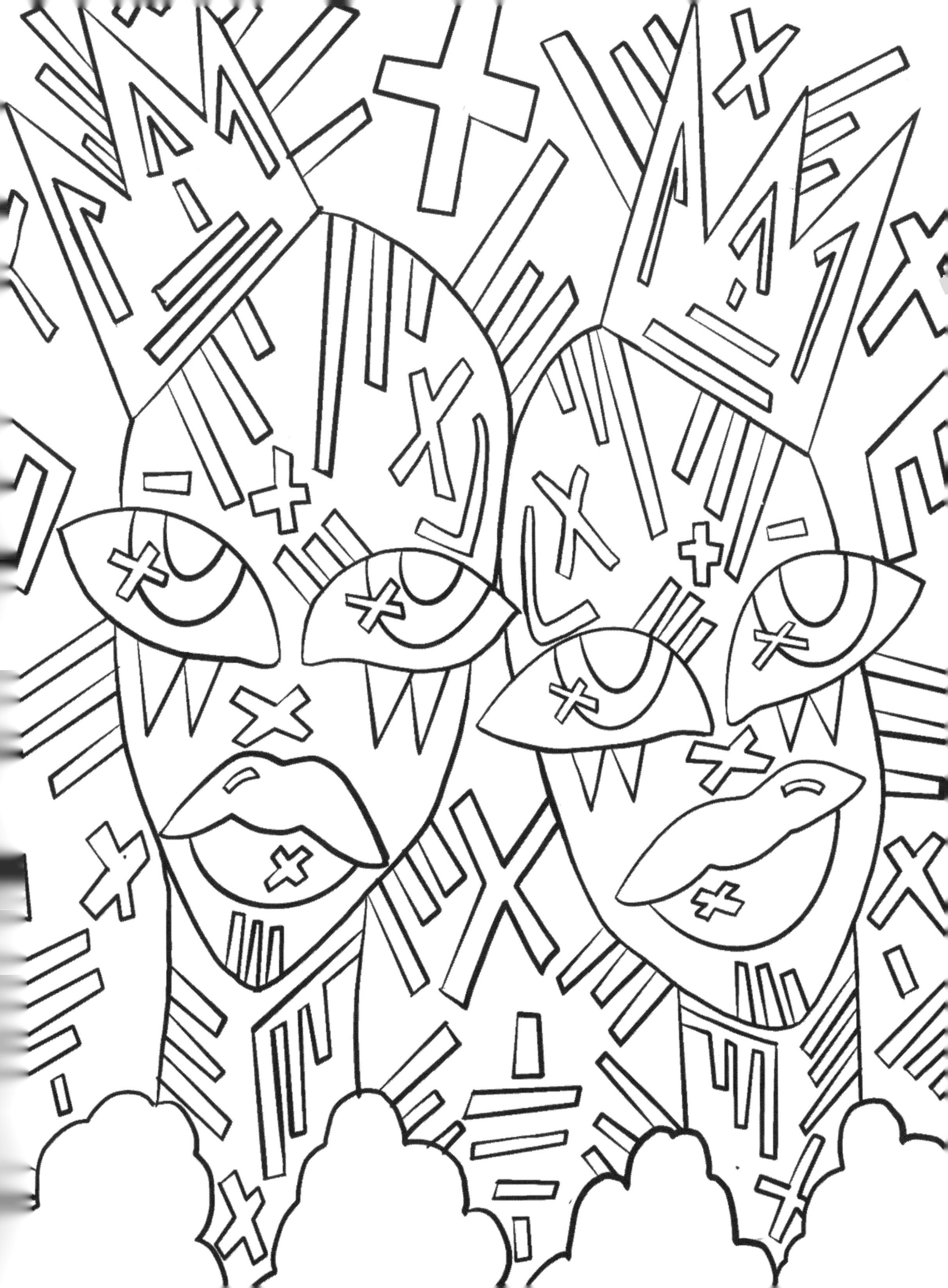

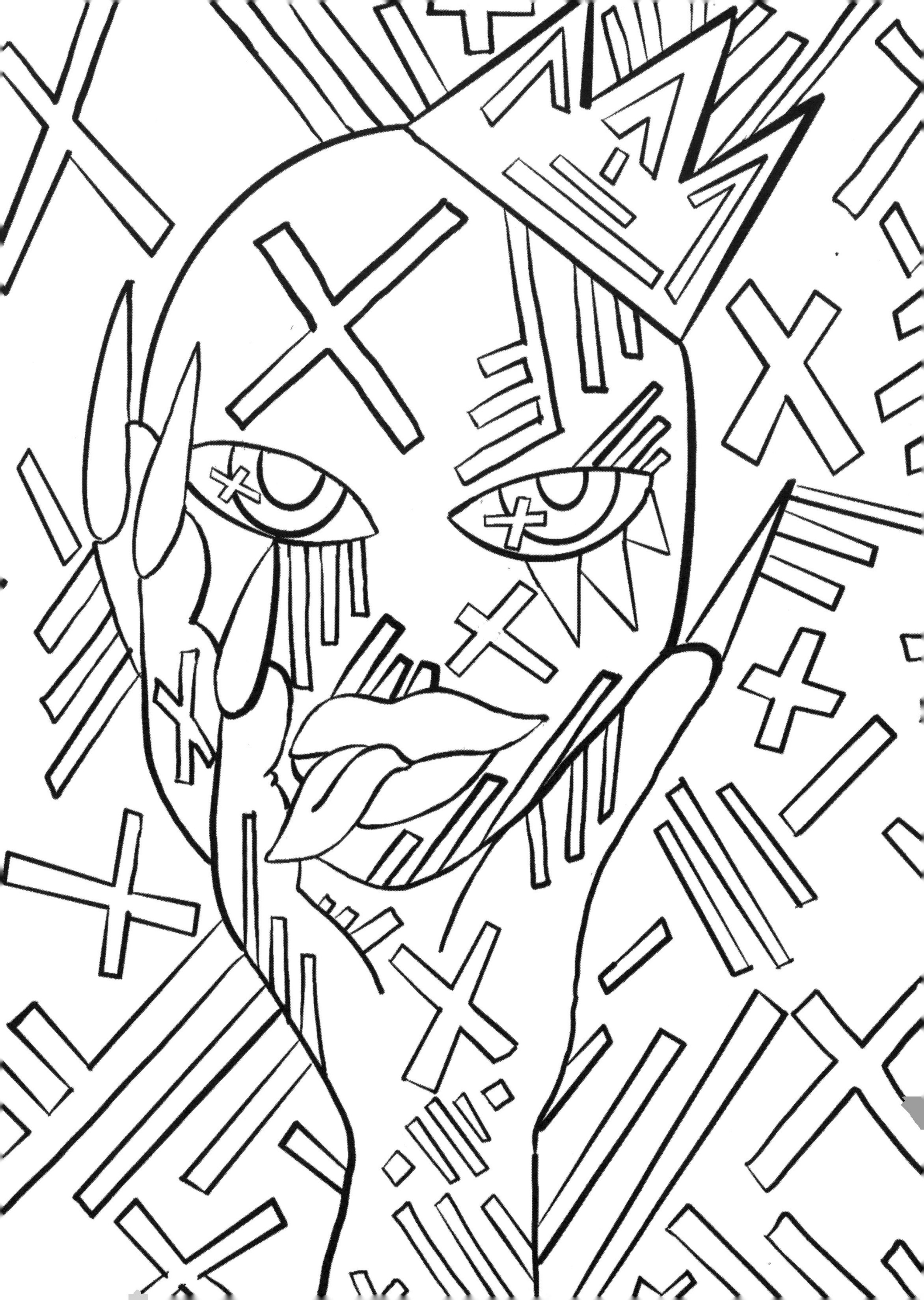

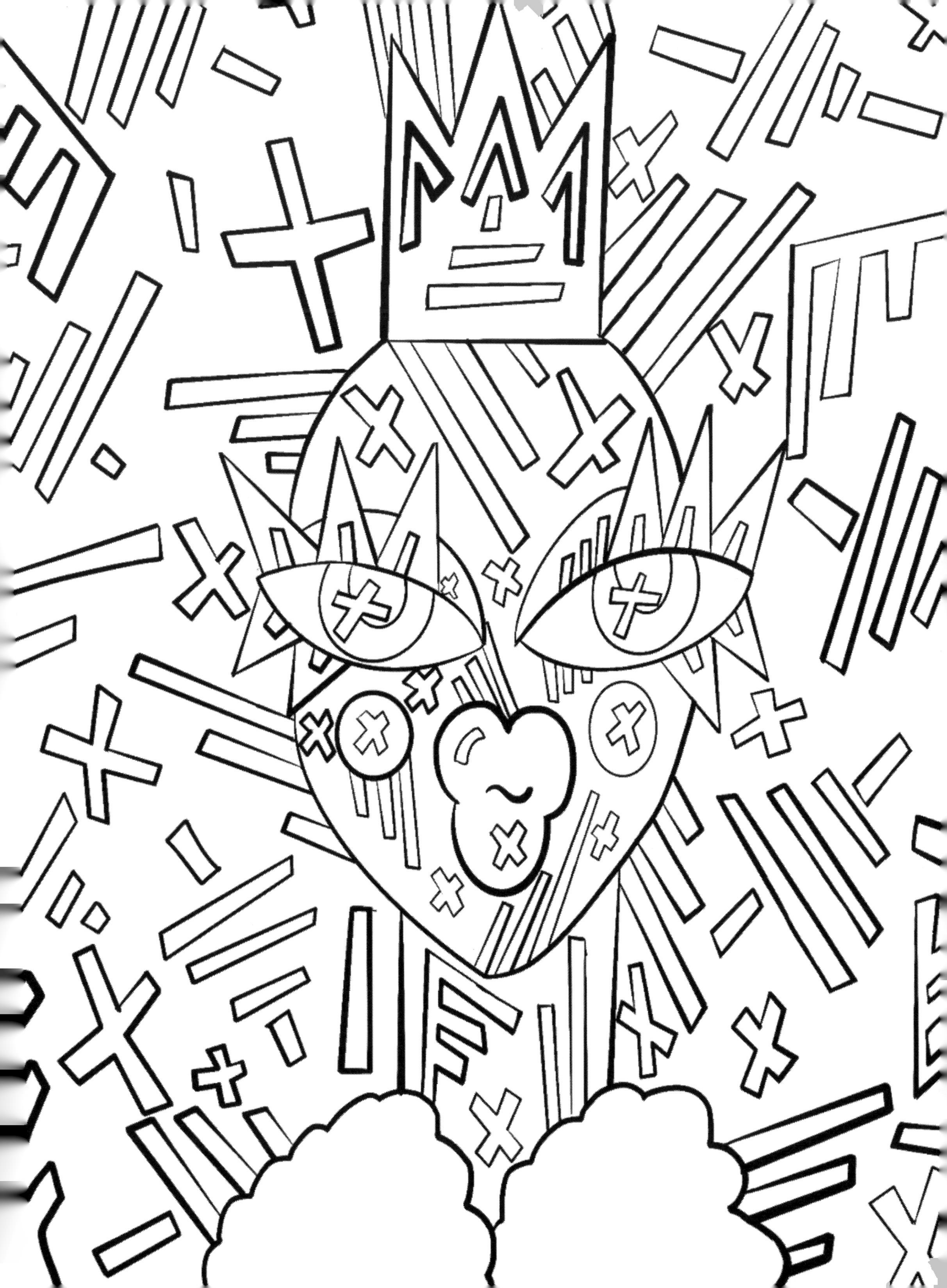

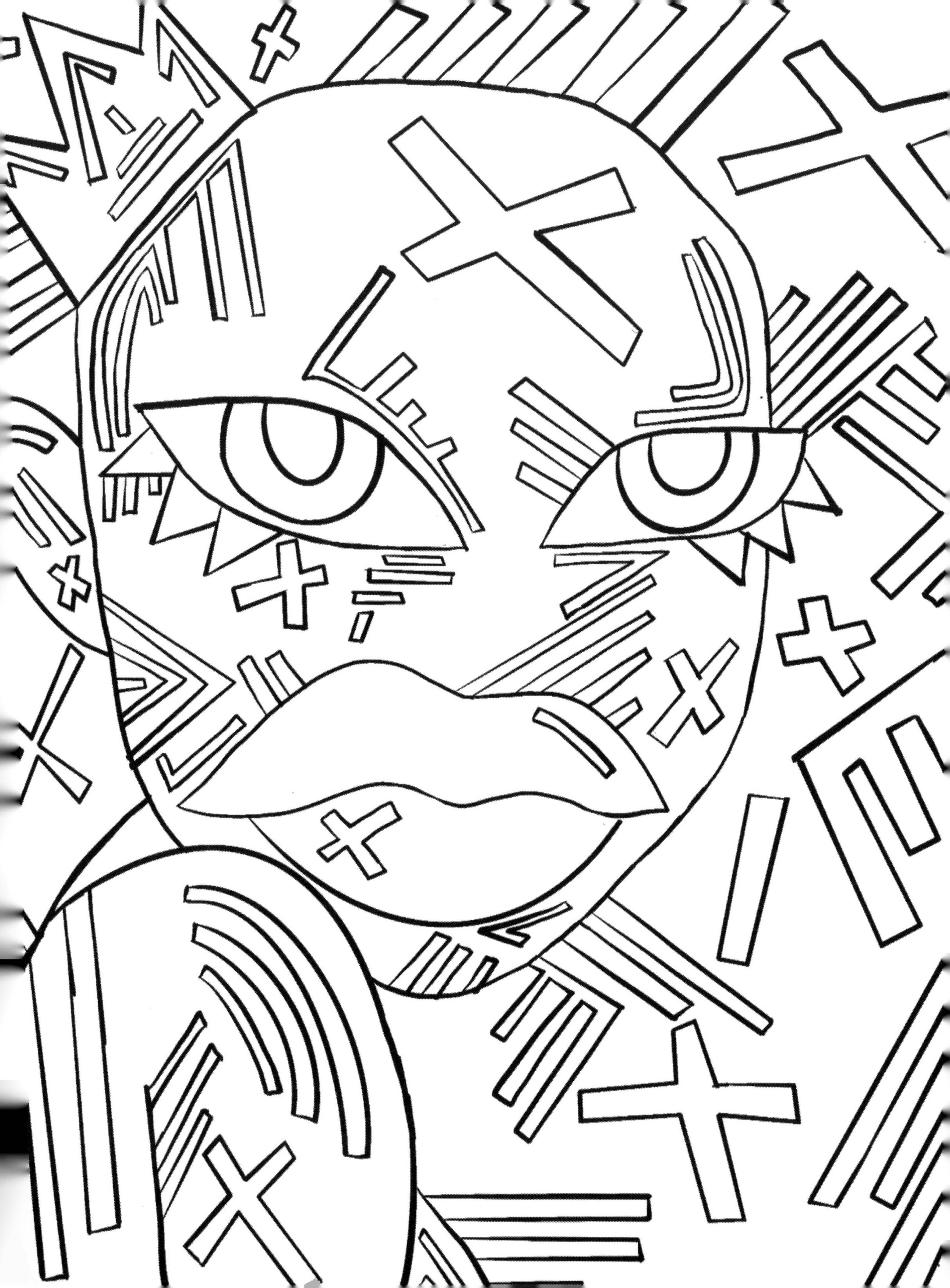

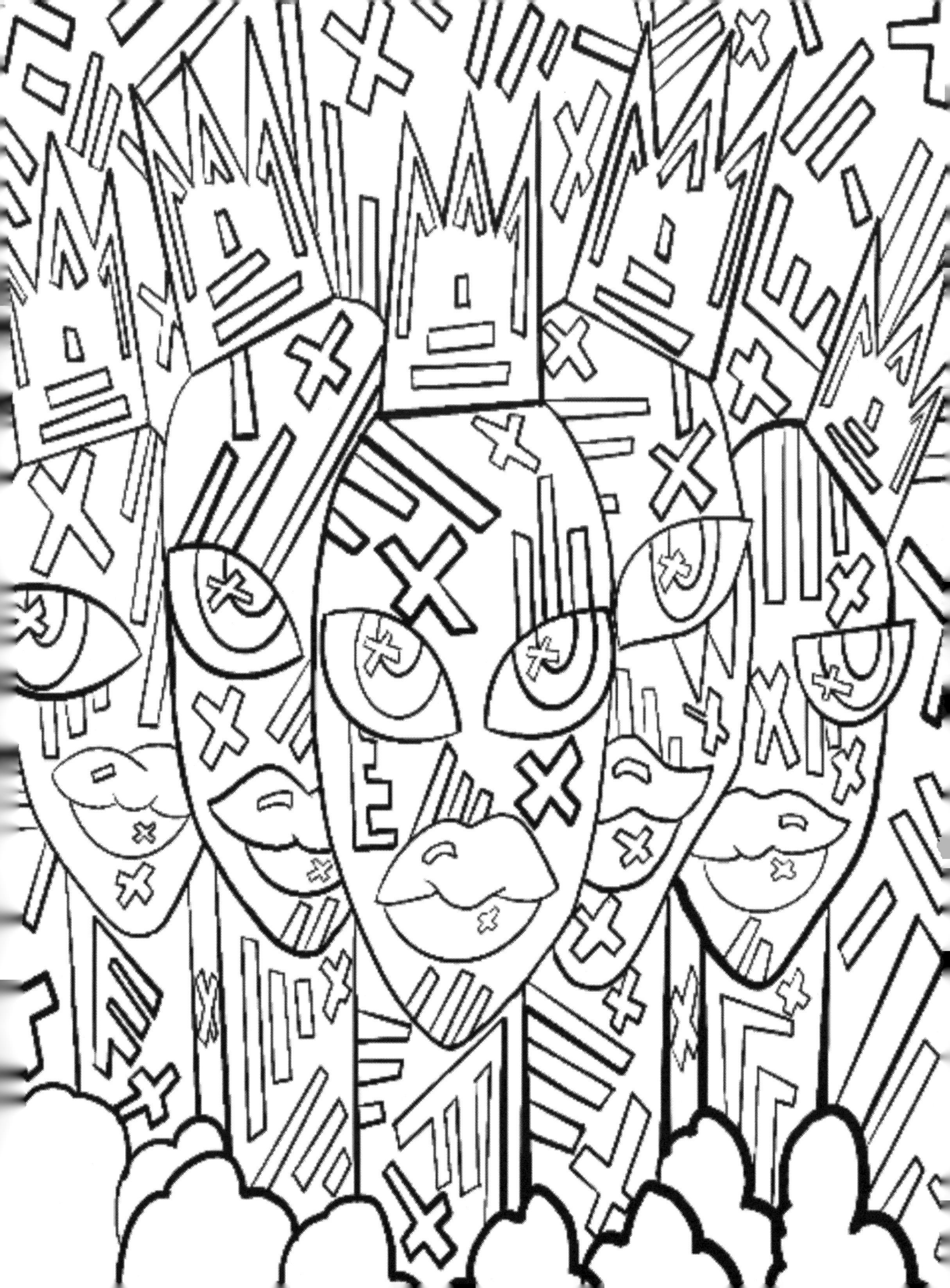

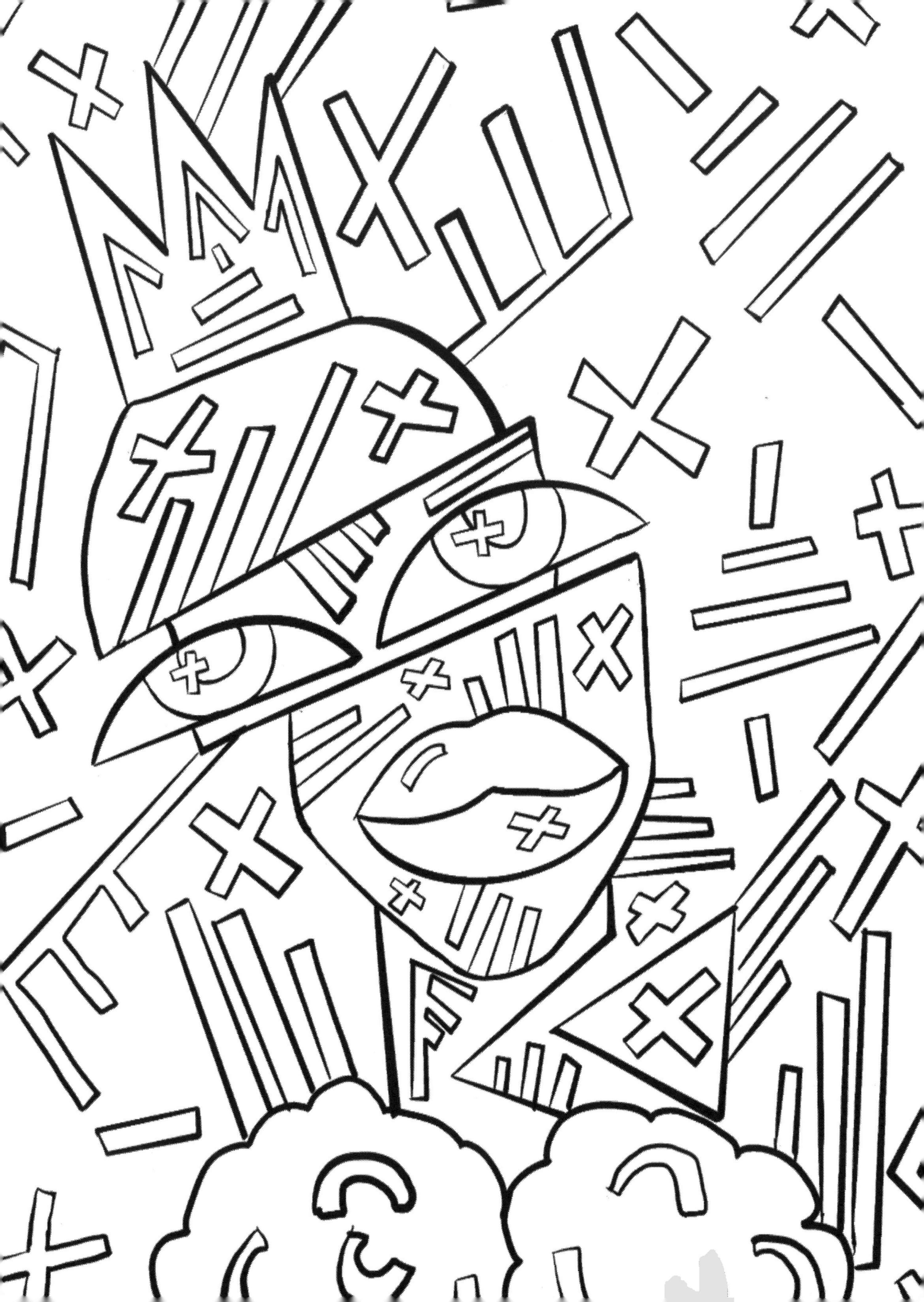

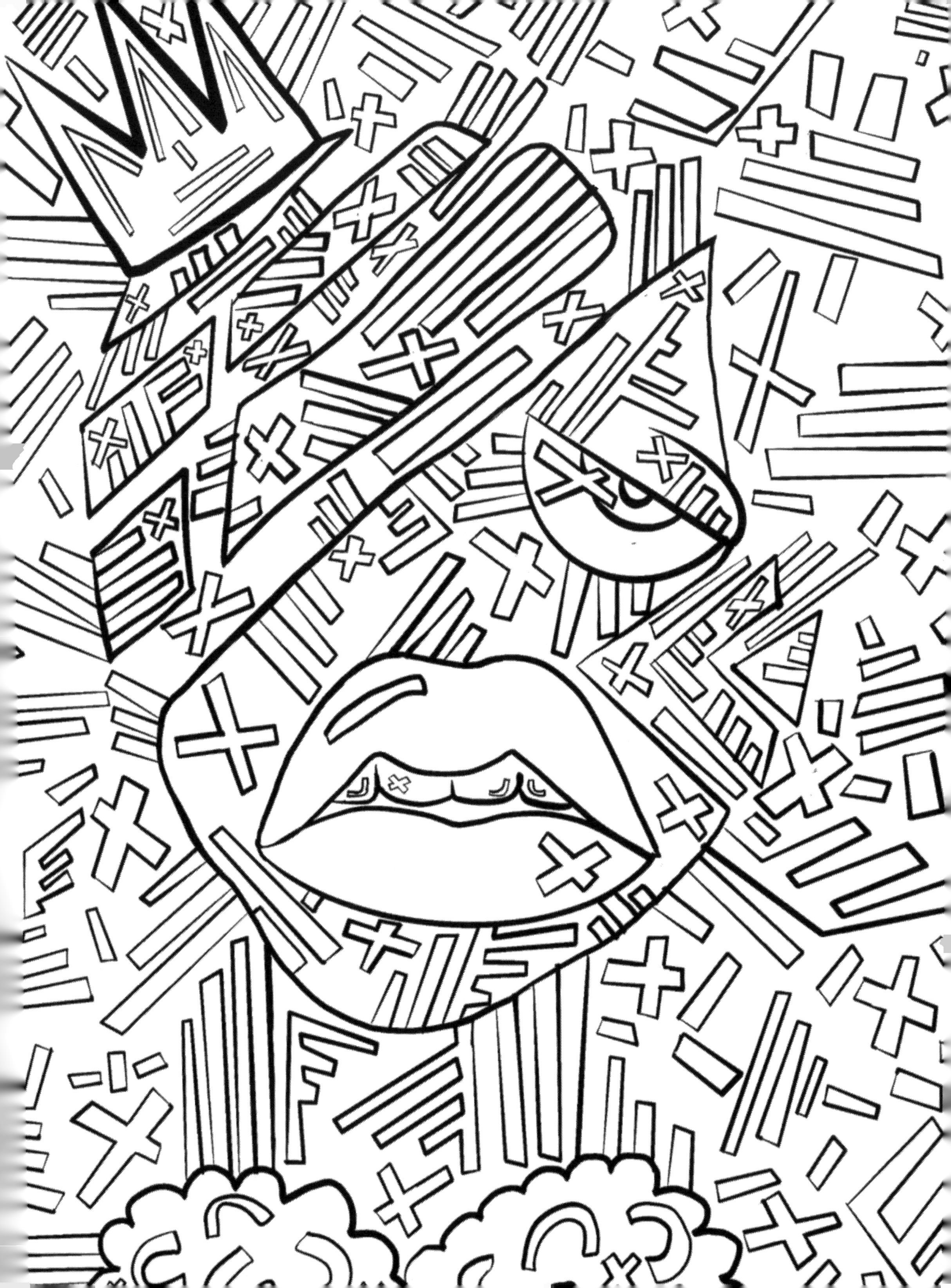

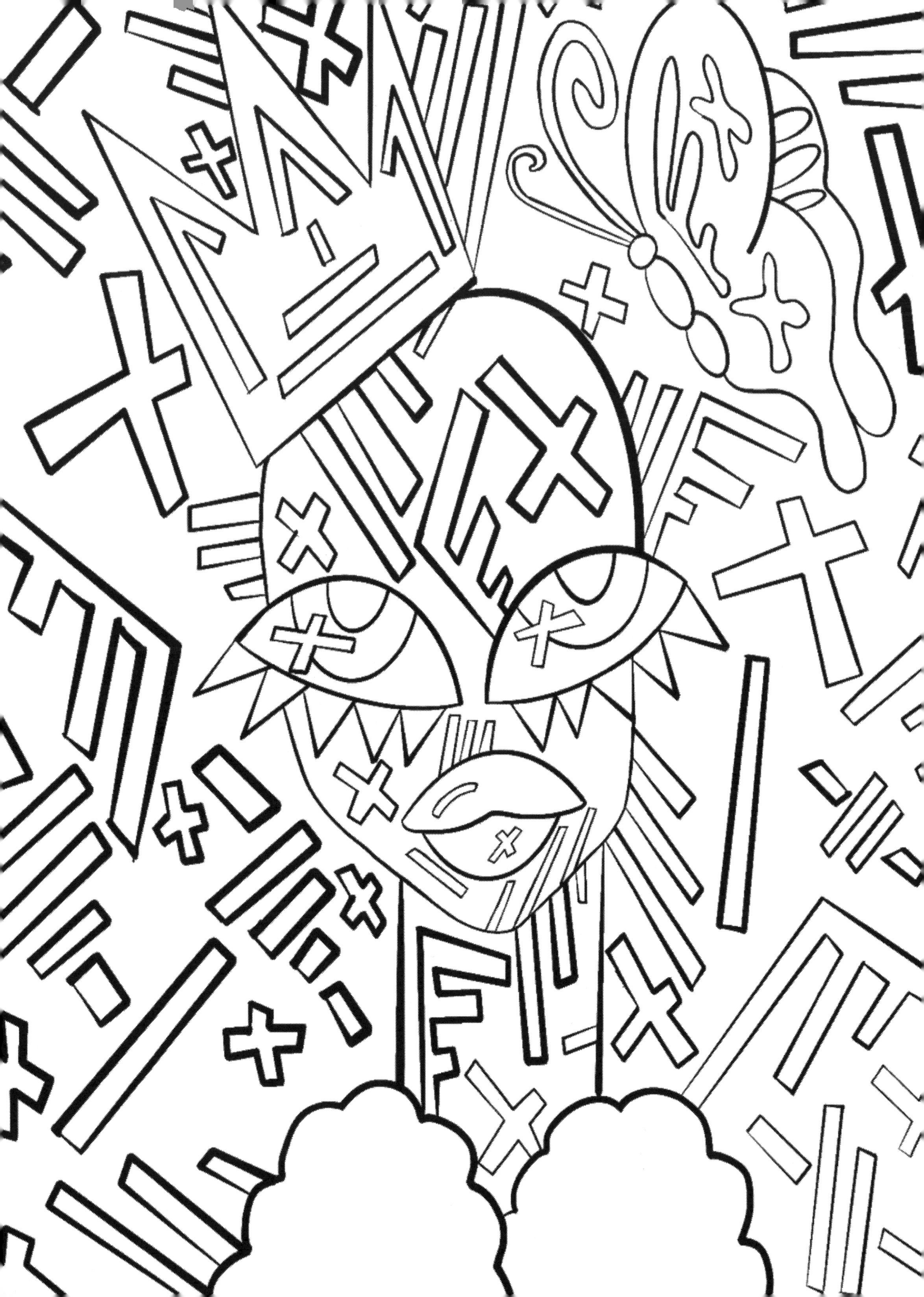

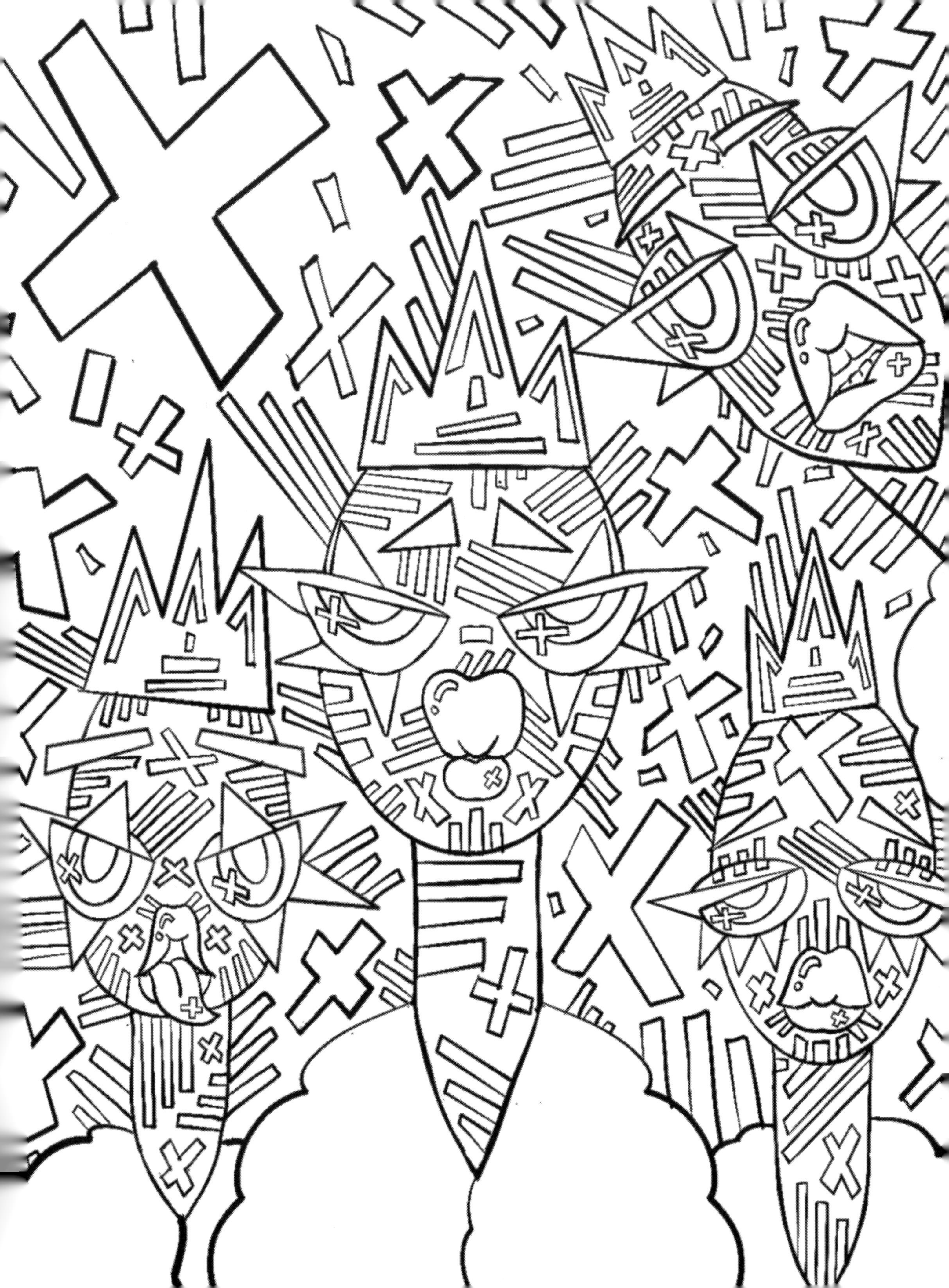

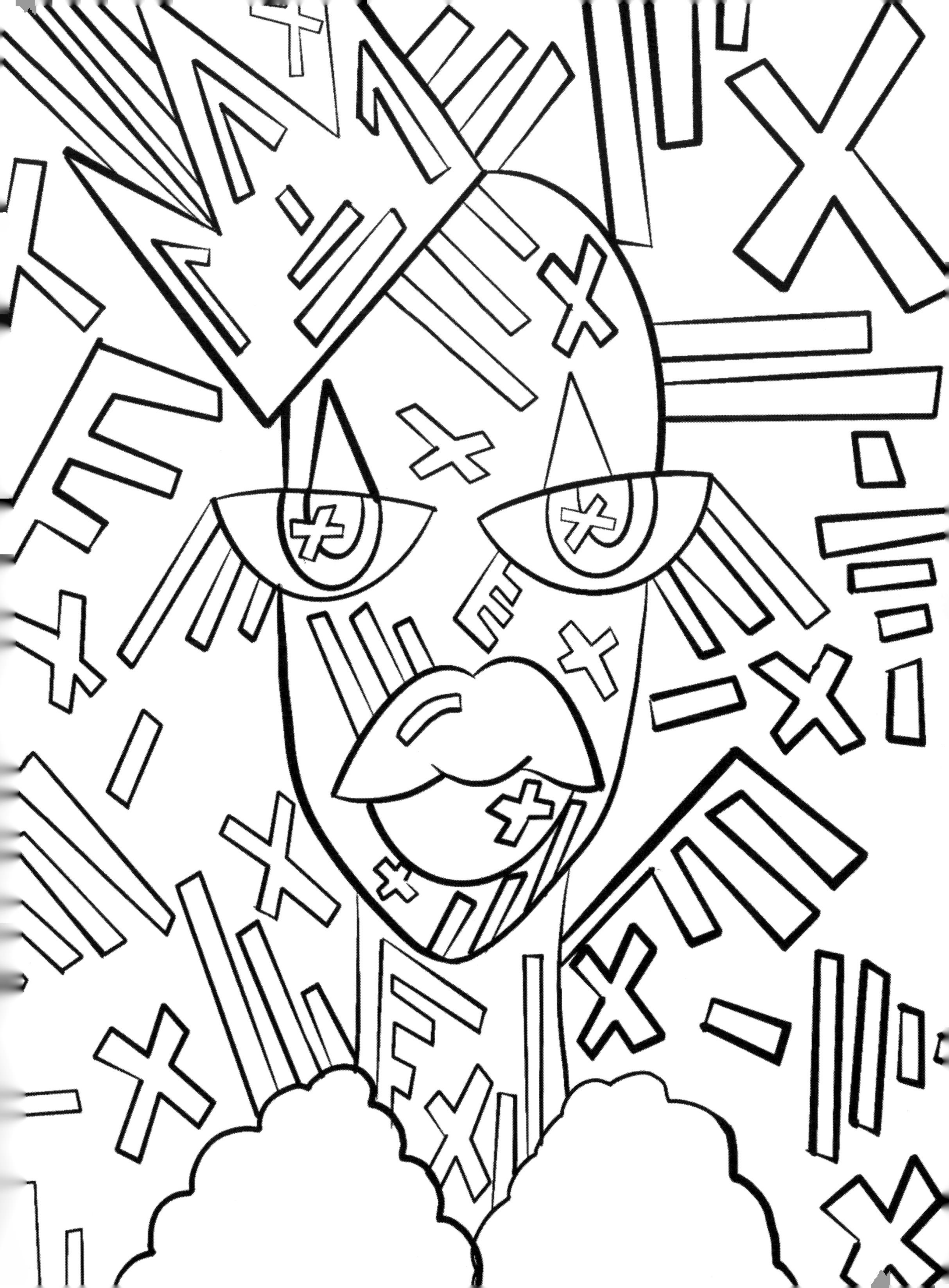

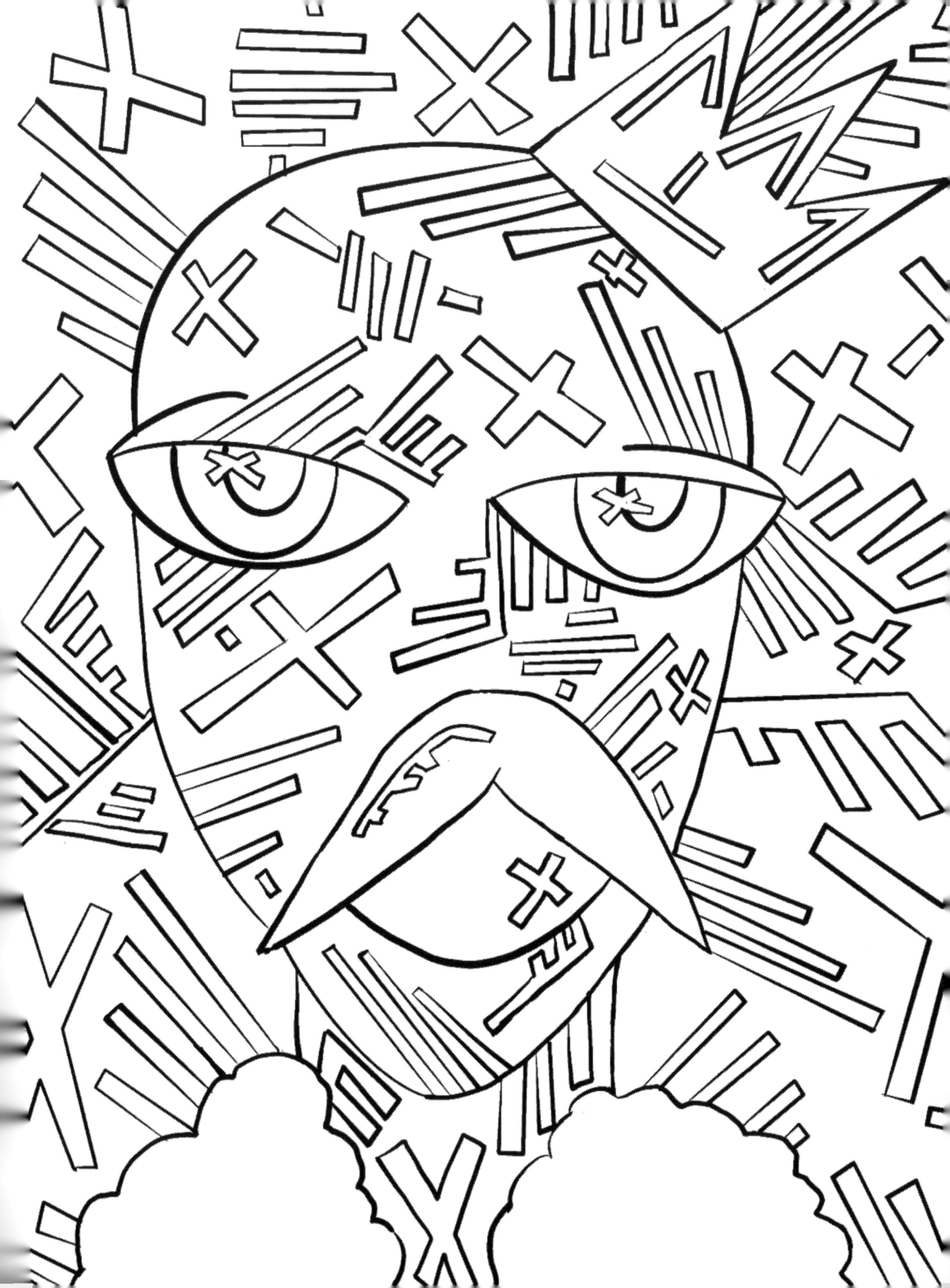

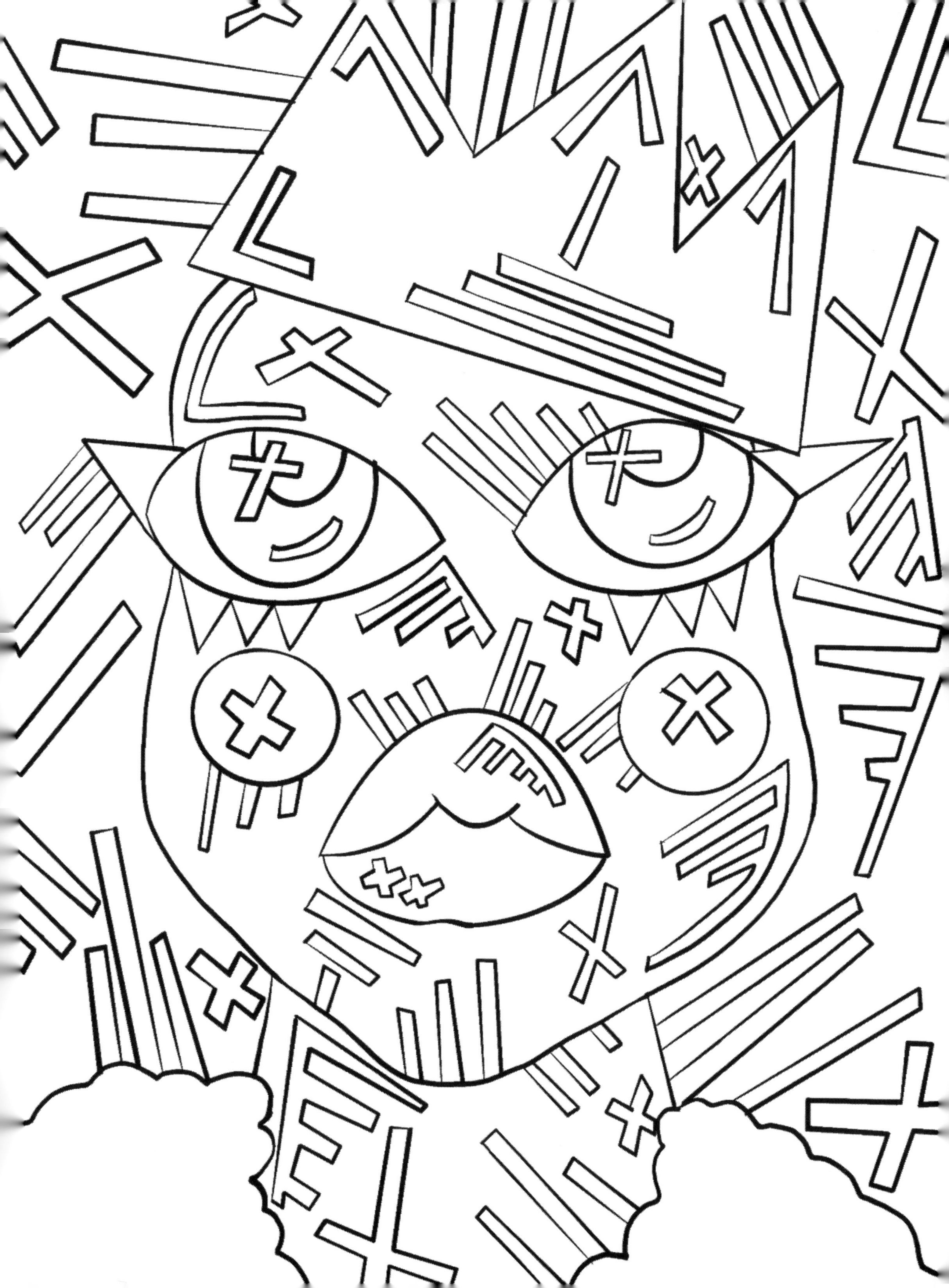

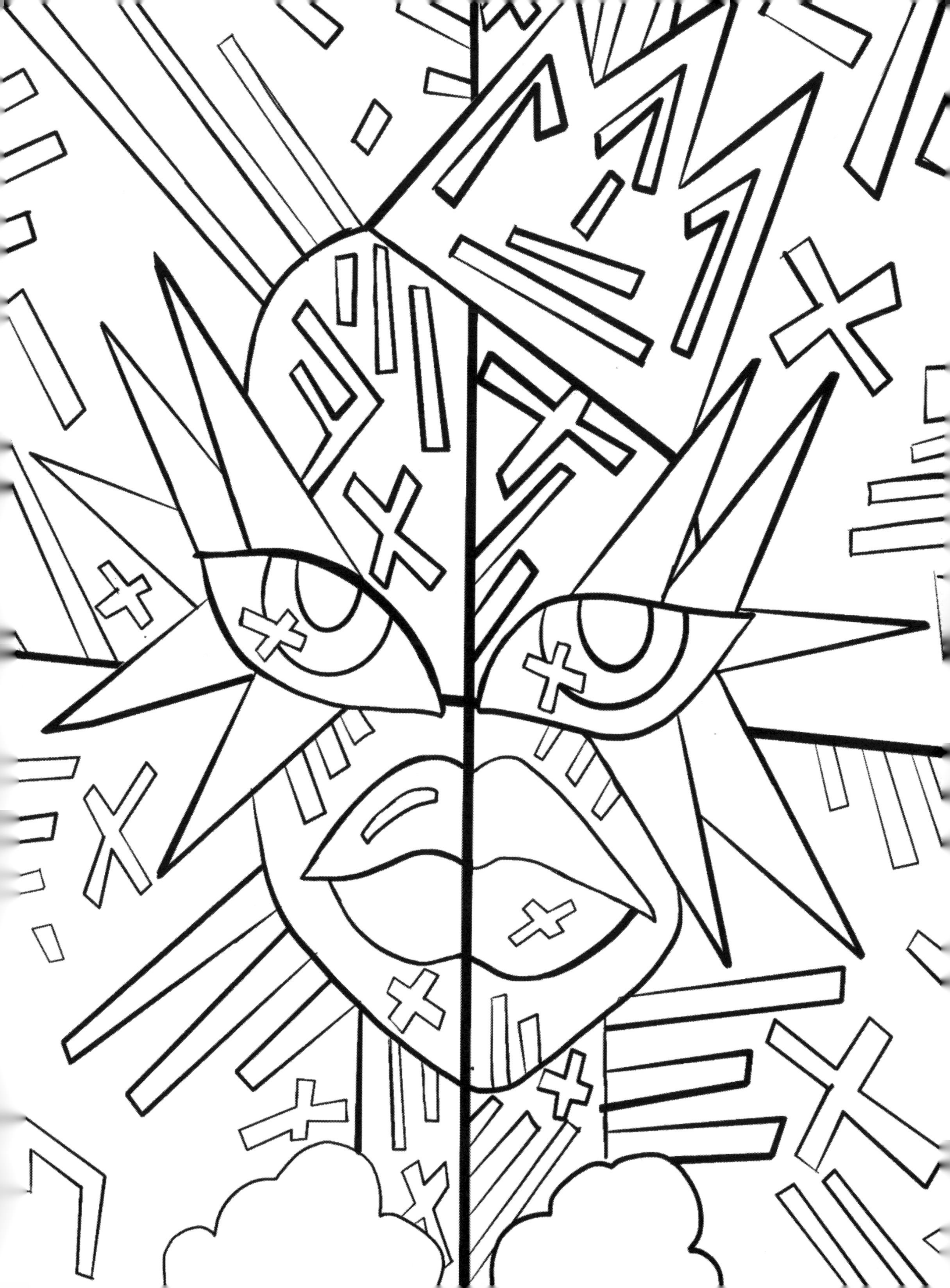

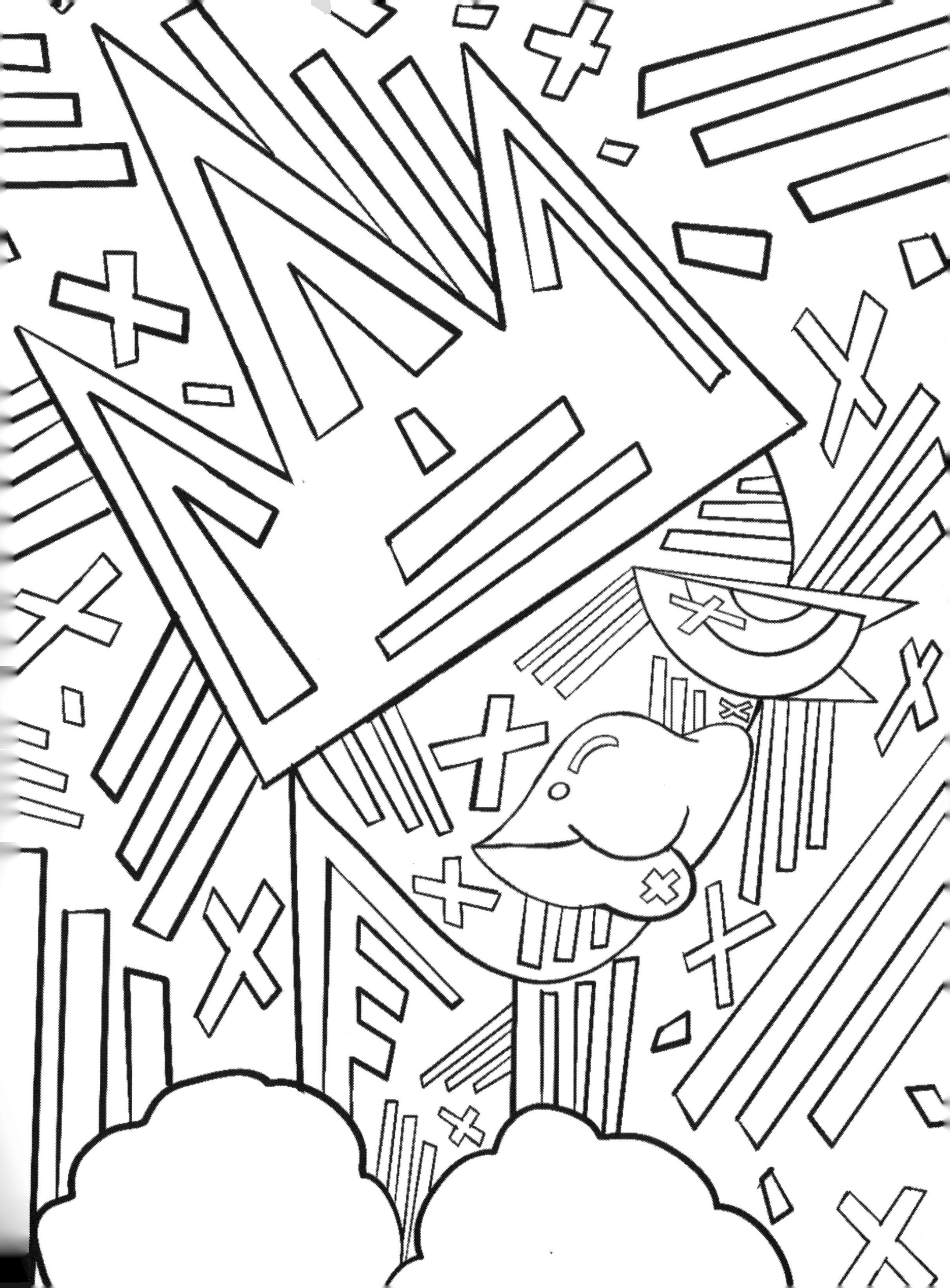

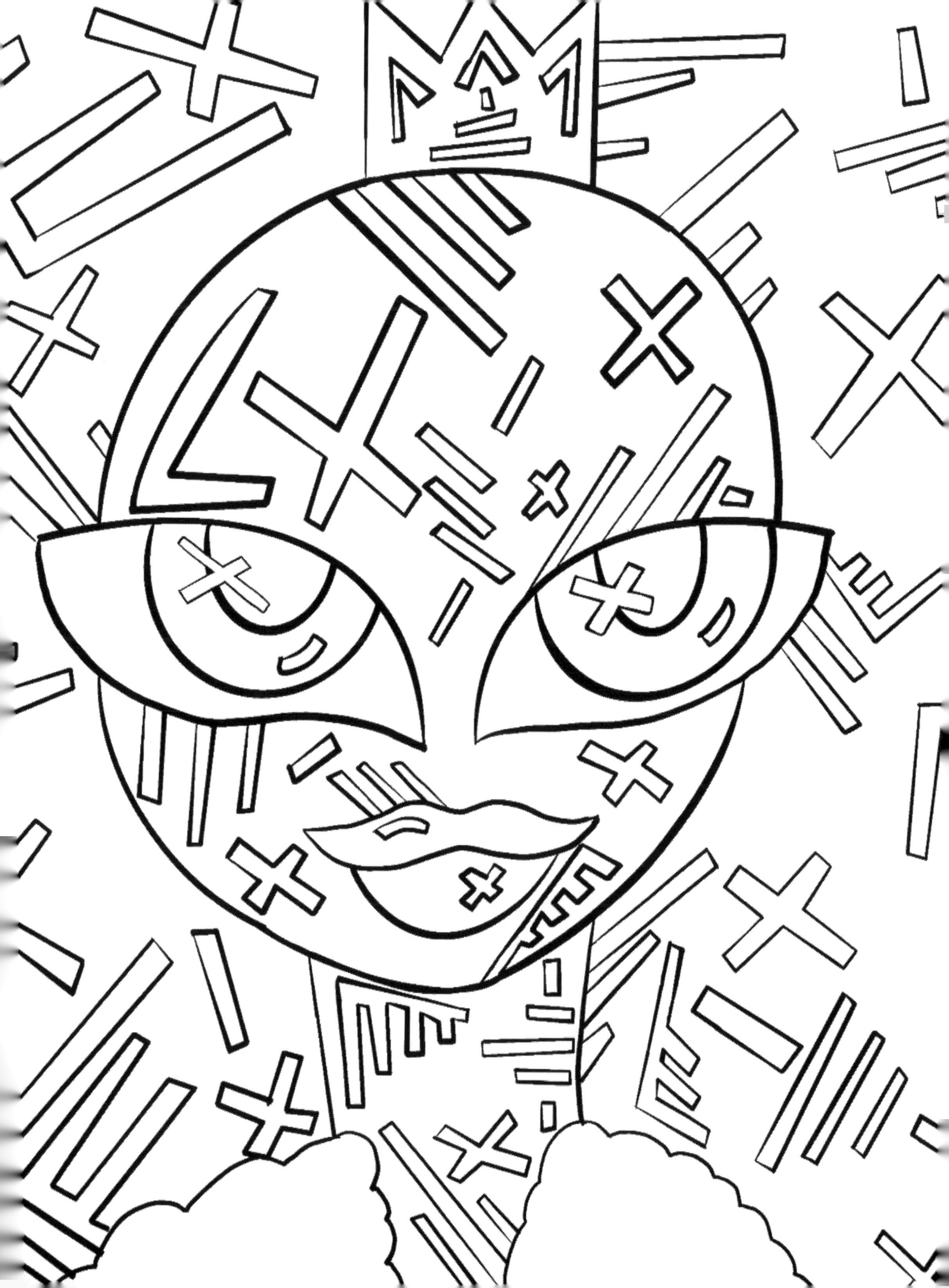

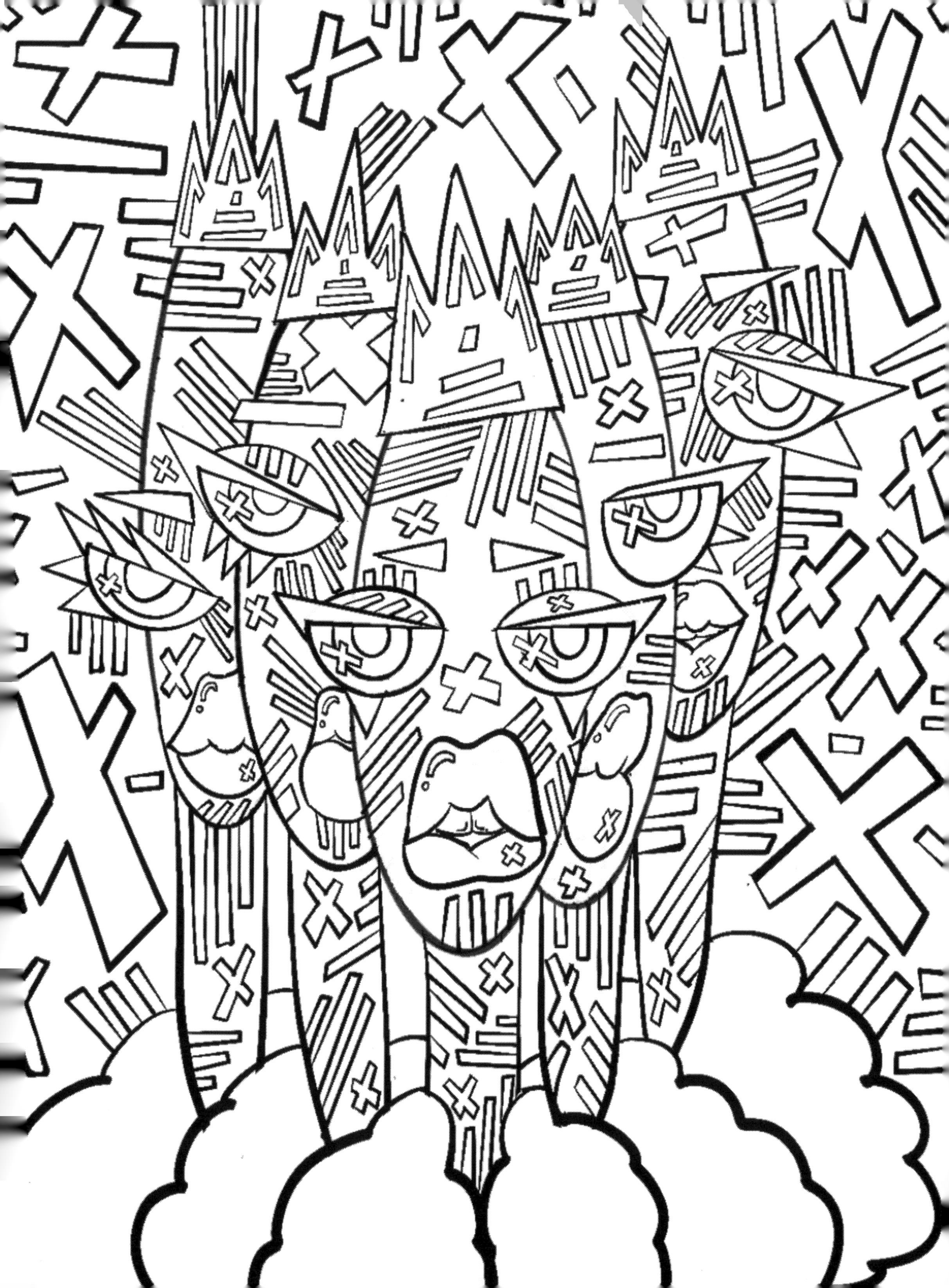

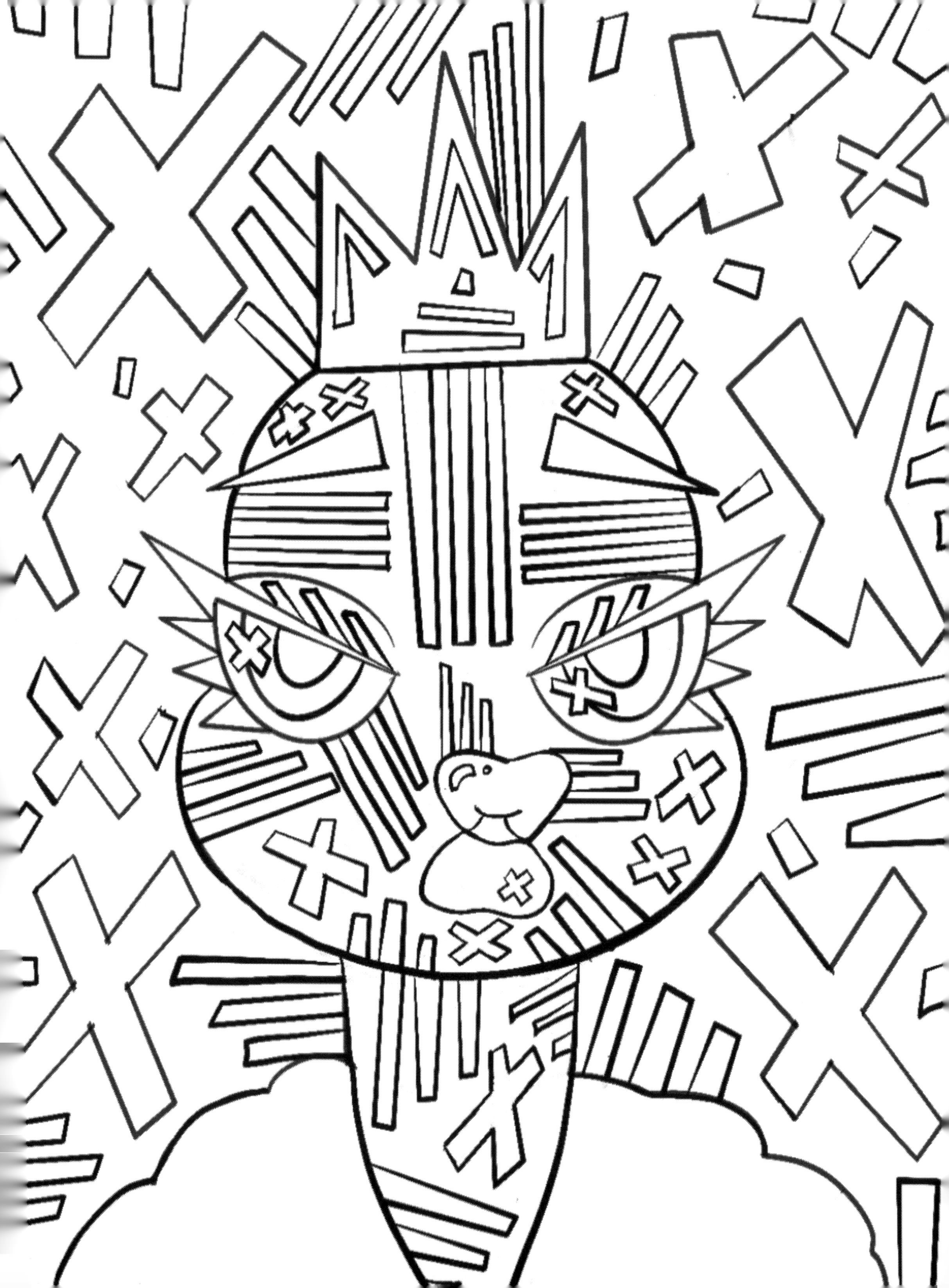

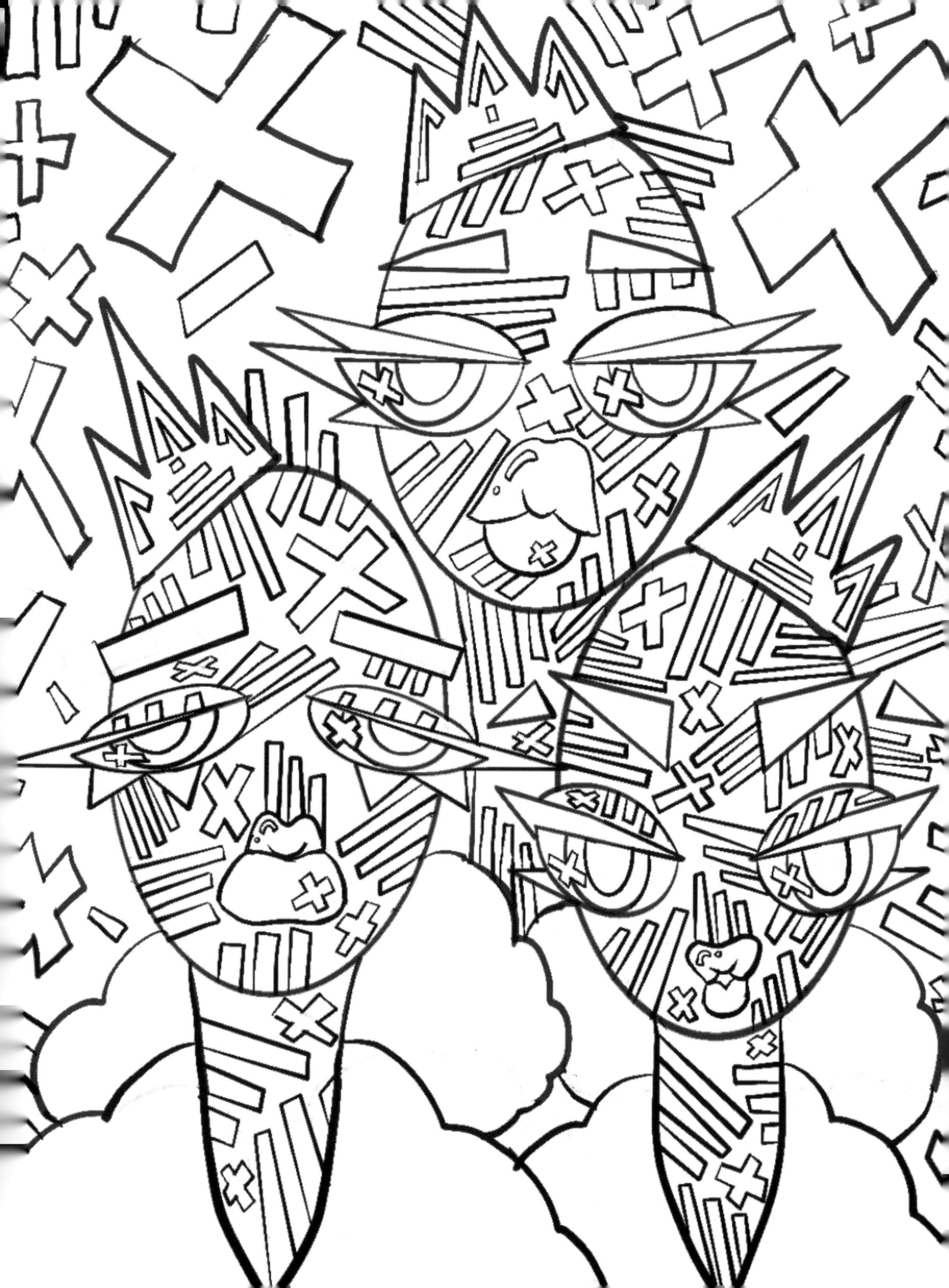

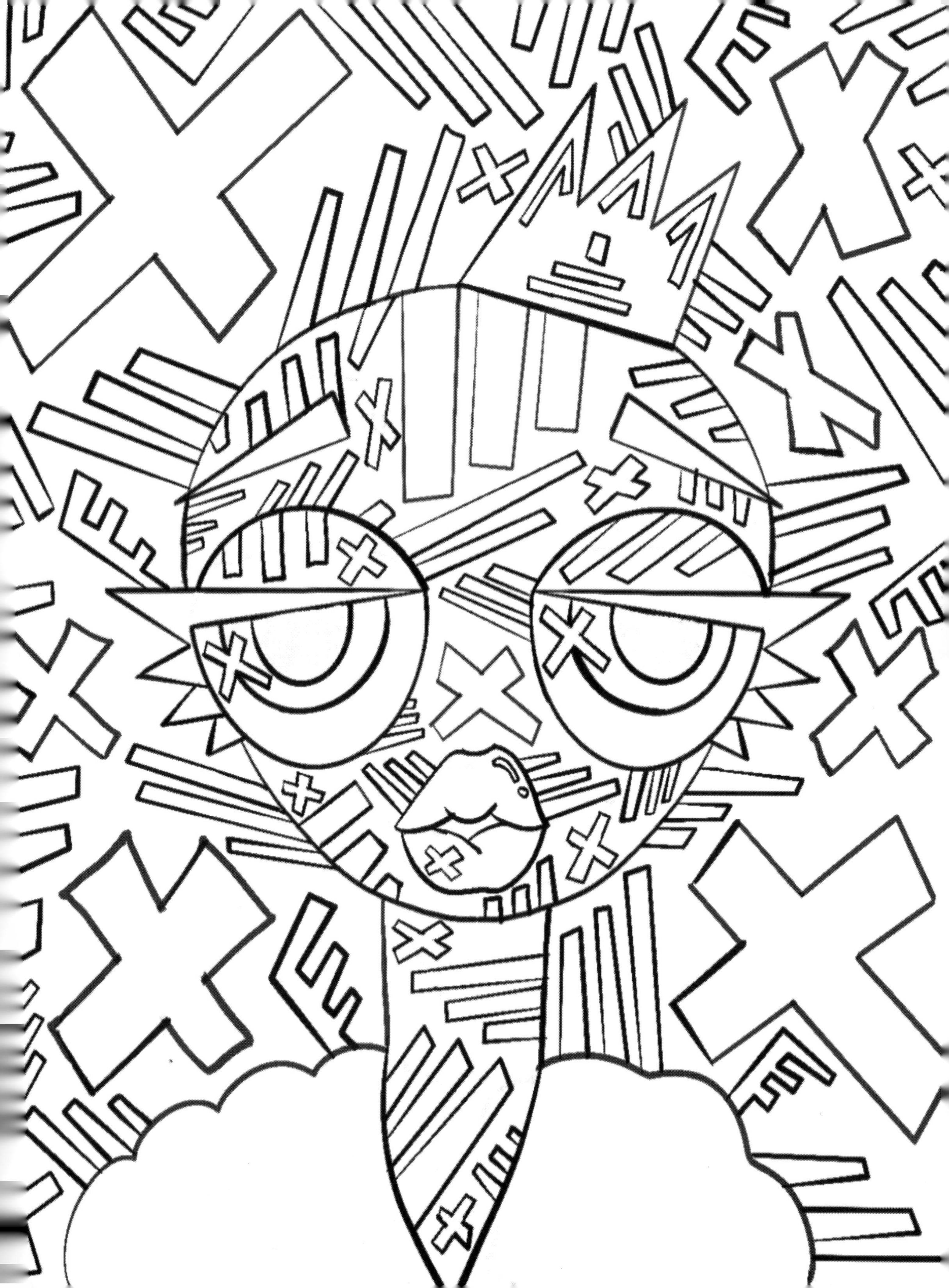

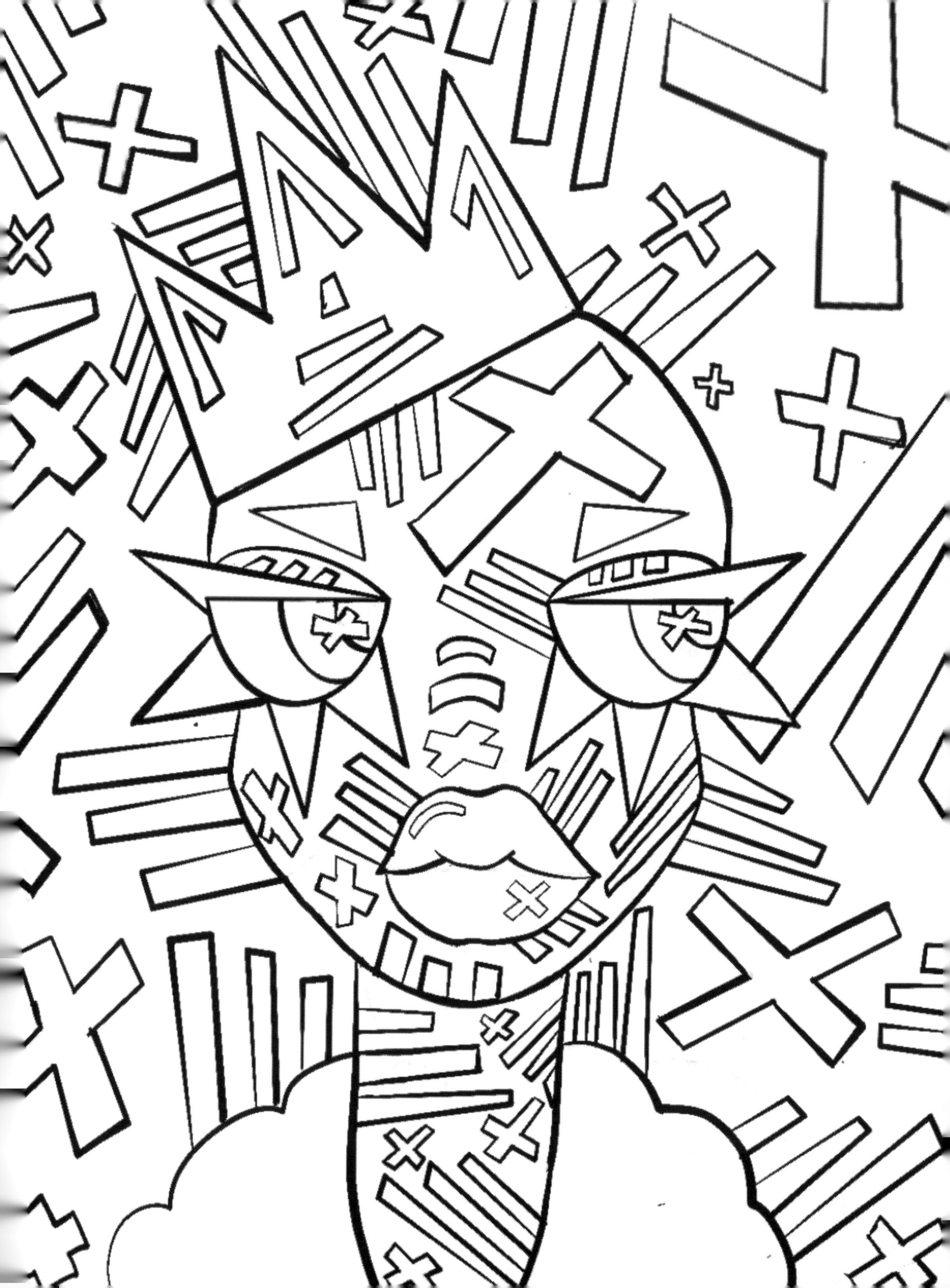

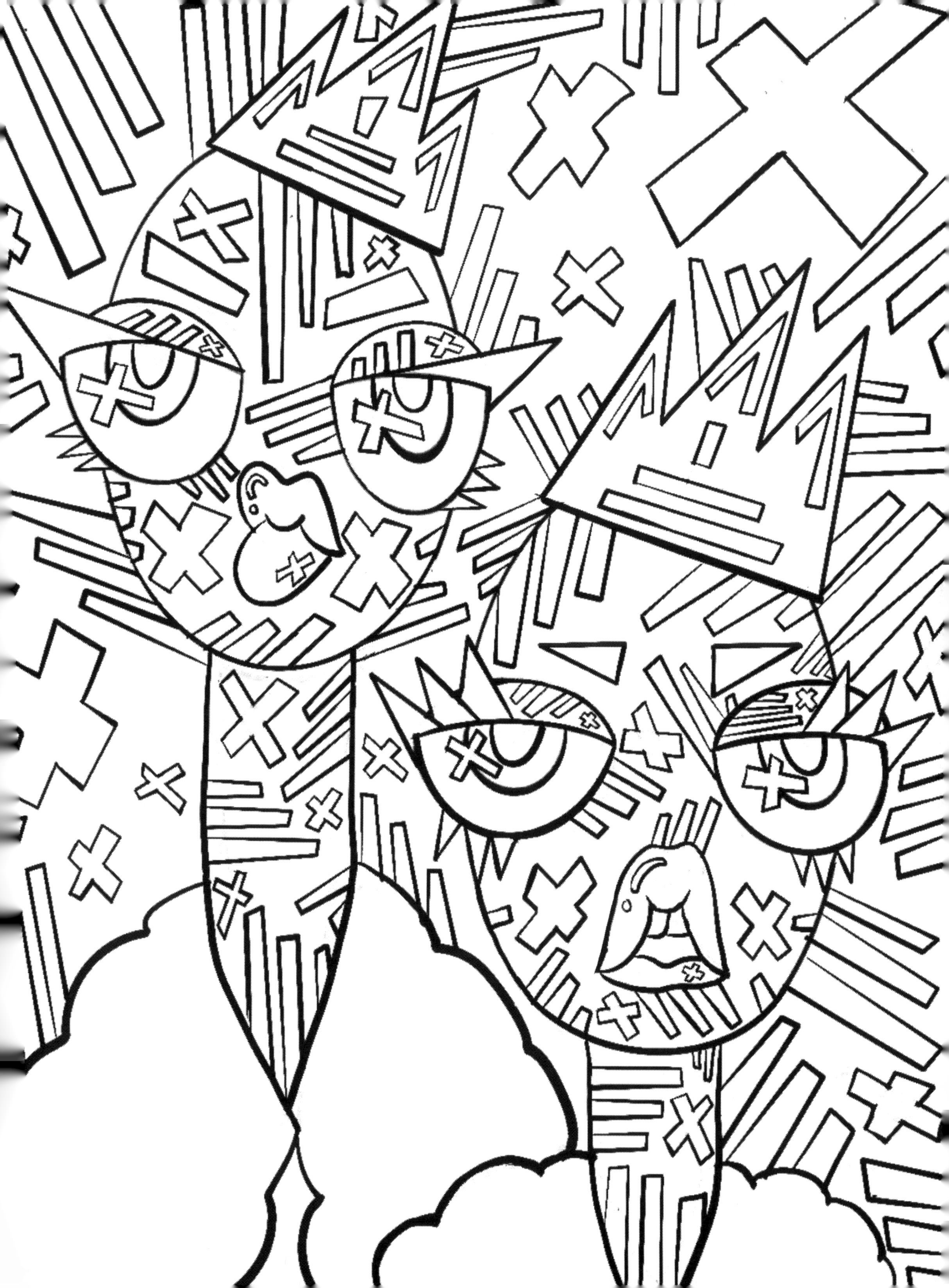

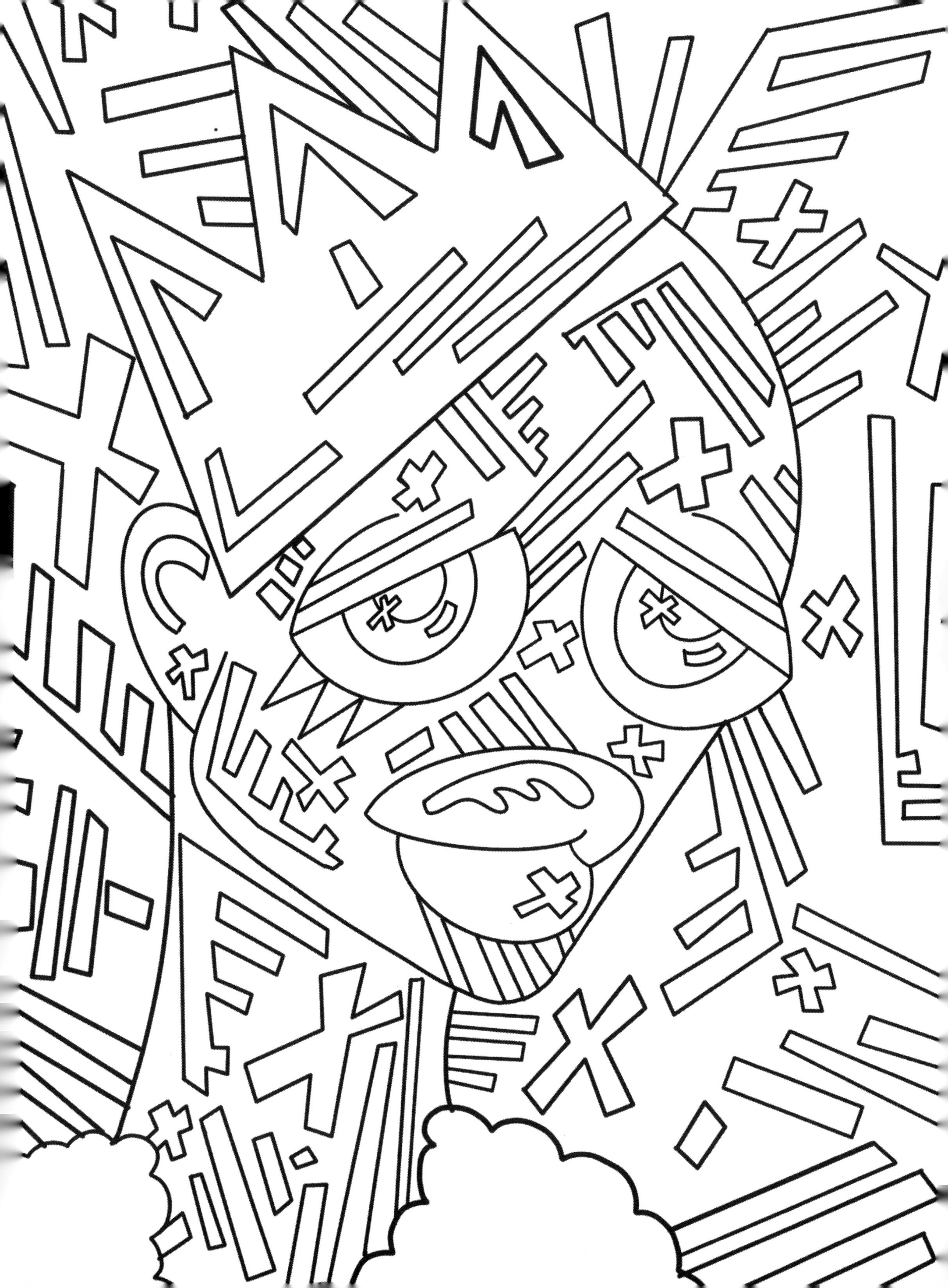

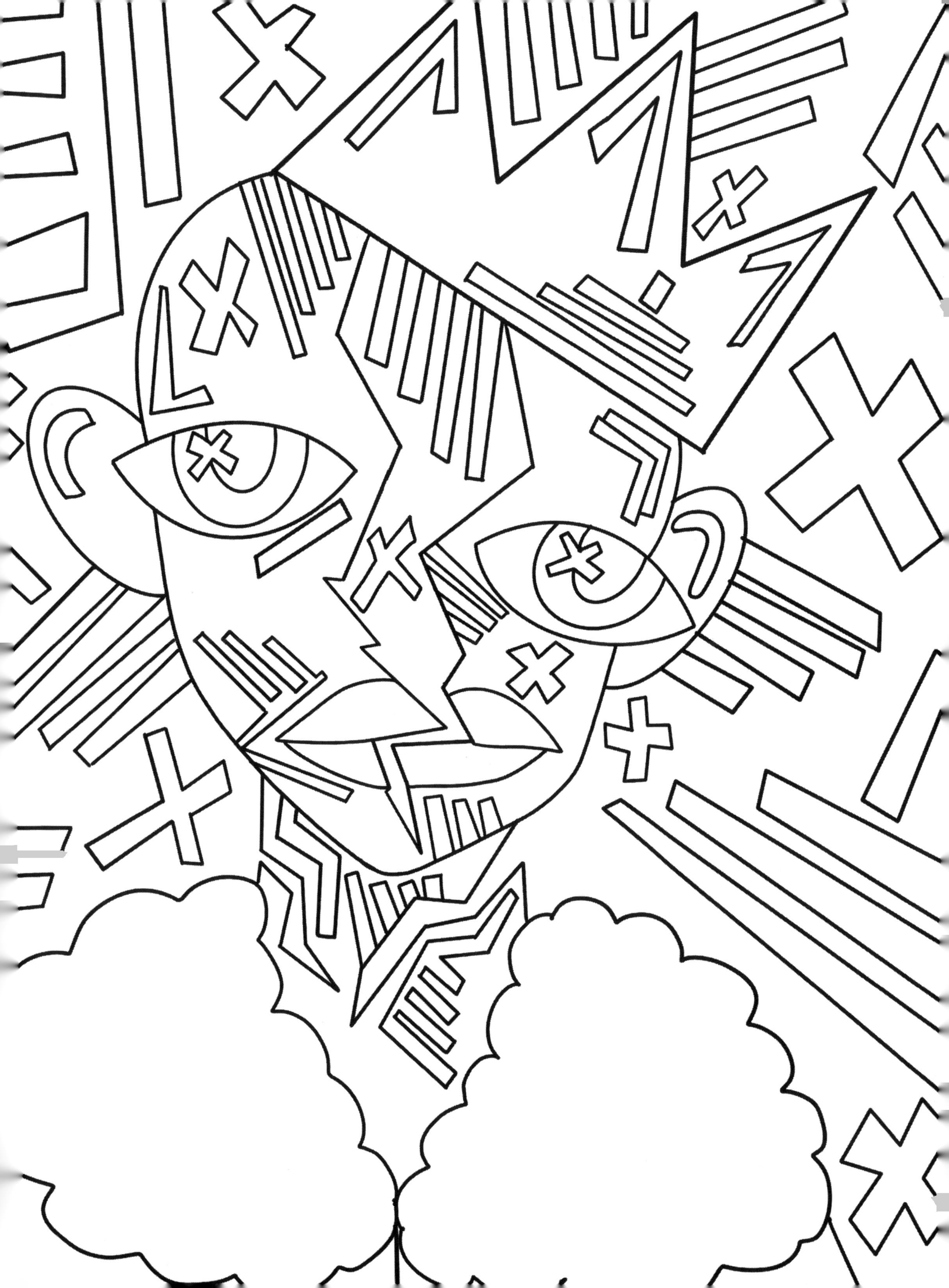

Made in the USA
Columbia, SC
21 October 2022

69783684R00026